Contents

Who were the Victorians?

The Victorians lived in Britain over 100 years ago. They were the millions of men, women and children who worked, studied, fought and played during the reign of Queen Victoria, who ruled Britain and its Empire between 1837 and 1901.

An industrial power

Victorian Britain was a time when industry and industrial towns grew very quickly. Politicians reformed Parliament and tried to improve the way British people lived. Scientists made many great discoveries, and Victorian engineers pioneered new inventions.

Britain became powerful and very rich. Together with other 'rival' European nations, Britain traded with and took control of foreign lands. By the end of Victoria's reign, Britain was the strongest and most confident nation in the world.

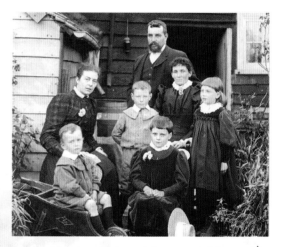

Hard working and respectable – a Victorian working-class family.

◀ The splendid new Victorian city hall, built in the prosperous industrial city of Leeds. It was opened by Queen Victoria in 1858.

The SS *Great Britain*, launched in 1843, was designed by the most famous Victorian engineer, Isambard Kingdom Brunel.

The *Great Britain* was the world's first ocean-going ship to be built of iron

A tall funnel carried away smoke from the ship's boilers, where water was heated by coal to produce steam

The *Great Britain* was also the world's first ocean-going ship to be driven through the water by a steam-powered propeller

How do we know?

Building Britain

Many Victorian factories, city halls, libraries, museums, railway stations and family houses, big and small, still survive in British towns. They tell us about the skill of the British working people, and how the Victorians lived.

Paintings and photographs

We know more about how people looked and how they dressed in Victorian times than in any other early century. Rich people paid for portraits to be painted. Both the rich and the poor also liked to have their images recorded by photography – a nineteenth-century invention.

Books and newspapers

New machines, invented by Victorians, made books, newspapers, advertising posters and all kinds of printed material cheaper than ever before. We can read these, and find out what Victorians thought and believed – and how they liked to spend their leisure time.

Queen and country

Victoria became queen in 1837, when she was just 18 years old. She ruled for an astonishing 63 years, longer than any other British monarch. When she died, in 1901, Britain was at the peak of its power.

A model for the nation

Queen Victoria did not make any of the decisions of government. That was the task of her Parliament and Prime Ministers. But she had a strong sense of duty and a keen interest in politics. She was brave (there were several attempts to kill her during her reign), hard working and determined. She had a very happy marriage, and a large, close-knit family.

Although Victoria was respected, her reign also saw many problems. Ordinary working people demanded better treatment by their employers and the right to vote in elections. Ireland (then ruled by Britain) demanded independence; women and religious minorities called for equal rights.

▲ Campaigners, such as Florence Nightingale, called for better care of the sick, and help for Britain's poor, homeless, old and unemployed people.

◀ The Houses of Parliament in London were rebuilt in grand style between 1835 and 1860.

Prince Albert Edward, known as 'Bertie', was Queen Victoria's oldest son. He became King Edward VII in 1901, when Victoria died

▲ Queen Victoria and Prince Albert (seated) with their first five children were pictured in this rich, glowing oil painting in 1848.

The Queen wears splendid jewels and a diamond tiara (lightweight crown)

Prince Albert wears evening dress and medals, given to him by Victoria

Princess Vicky, Queen Victoria's oldest daughter, became her trusted friend

Protesters and campaigners

- 1796–1858 Socialist Robert Owen runs pioneer Co-operative community. He uses profits from his factories to improve workers' lives.

- 1832 Parliamentary elections are reformed. For the first time, middle-class men with property get the vote.

- 1838–1948 'Chartist' mass protests demand votes for all adult men and more parliamentary reform.

- 1842 New laws allow Trades Union protests. Members demand better pay and safer working conditions.

- 1844 First workers' Co-operative shares trading, educational and welfare benefits.

- 1850–1900 Many thousands of men (and, later, women) join Trades Unions.

- 1864 First International (a Communist workers' association) set up.

- 1867 and 1884 Working-class men get the vote.

- 1897 National Union of Suffrage Societies starts to campaign for votes for women.

Make a top hat

During the reign of Queen Victoria, it became fashionable for wealthy men to wear tall hats, called top hats, which were made from stiff felt, beaver fur or silk. One version of the top hat was nicknamed the 'stovepipe' hat. This type of hat was taller and straighter than an ordinary top hat and became especially popular in the United States.

Victorian clothes

Victorian clothes for wealthy people – especially for women and girls – must have been very uncomfortable. Women wore corsets made out of whale bone that were pulled really tight with laces to make waists seem tiny. They also wore heavy petticoats and, in the 1850s and 1860s, a large frame of steel hoops, called a crinoline, to make their skirts stick out. Men usually wore suits, with long frock coats. Children were usually dressed like their parents.

Most Victorian people ▶ wore hats. Tall top hats for men became very fashionable after 1850, when Queen Victoria's husband, Prince Albert, first wore one in public.

1

Measure around your head. Add a extra 2cm, then cut out a piece of black card that width and around 30cm tall. Glue the long edges together to make a cylinder.

4

To make the brim, draw around a large dinner plate on black card and cut it out. Place the cylinder in the centre and draw around it. Draw another circle 1.5–2cm inside this pencil circle and cut around that line. Snip notches from the middle to the pencil line, fold down and glue to the cylinder.

2

Place the cylinder on a sheet of black card and draw around it. Cut out a circle that is 1.5–2cm larger than the cylinder circle. Below: snip notches from the edge of the card to the cylinder pencil line at regular intervals.

3

Fold down the notches and glue the flaps inside the cylinder to make the top of your hat.

Glue a strip of black felt or a piece of ribbon, to neaten the edges and strengthen the join

Glue another strip of black felt or a piece of ribbon at the base of the cylinder

You will need

- Pencil • Tape measure
- Craft glue • Scissors
- Large dinner plate
- Black cardboard
- Black ribbon or felt

Workshop of the world

In Queen Victoria's reign, Britain became the world's leading industrial nation. It grew rich by mass-producing cloth, pottery, glass, ironwork and many other goods using new, steam-powered machines.

Factories and coal mines

Before this 'Industrial Revolution' people made clothes, tools and other objects at home or in small workshops. After 1750, British businessmen built huge factories to house new pumps, weaving looms and many other machines, designed by British inventors. Coal from new mines was used to heat water to make steam, for blast furnaces and foundries to produce cast iron.

▲ Massive machines, such as this steam-hammer, invented in 1839 by James Nasmyth, made panels for ships, iron building materials and parts for tools.

These machines could make goods far more quickly and cheaply than home-workers, but they still needed people to operate them. Thousands of families left their homes in the countryside, to live in new towns that grew up close to factories.

The Crystal Palace, in London, was built ▶ in 1851 to house a 'Great Exhibition of Arts and Manufactures', organised by Victoria's husband, Prince Albert.

Driving belt carries power from steam-engine

Huge bobbins (spools) of cotton thread, ready to be threaded on looms

Finished cloth is wound on huge rollers

▲ Cloth-making factories employed men, women and children. Cotton cloth became Britain's leading machine-made product, and British cotton goods were traded all over the world.

Young girl collects empty bobbins (spools)

Women workers manage steam-powered looms that weave cloth

A young girl crawls under moving machinery to check for broken threads

Railways and steamships

New railways and steamships carried British factory-made goods to buyers all round the world. Railways also carried farm produce from the British countryside to feed factory workers in towns.

- 1804 World's first steam-powered railway locomotive, designed by Richard Trevithick, starts work in South Wales.
- 1825 First public passenger railway built, from Stockton to Darlington.

- 1829 George Stephenson builds fast, reliable 'Rocket' locomotive.
- 1838 SS *Great Western*, designed by Isambard Kingdom Brunel, is first steamship regularly to cross the Atlantic Ocean.
- 1843 Brunel builds fast, efficient SS *Great Britain*, the first steamship driven by a propeller made of iron.
- 1860 Almost 10,000km of railways in Britain.
- 1863 First underground railway, in London.
- 1870 More than 24,000km of railways in Britain.

Make a loom

Before the Industrial Revolution, people spun thread and wove cloth at home on hand-powered machines, such as spinning wheels and looms. After the invention of steam-driven machines, cloth was produced in huge factories and mills. This project shows you how to make a simple, cardboard-box loom, so you can see how thread can be woven into cloth.

Child labour

Compared with today, Victorian factory owners paid their workers low wages in order to keep costs down and make a bigger profit. This meant that whole families, including young children, had to work long hours to earn enough money for food. Children were often employed in mills and cloth-making factories because they were small enough to crawl under the machines. As the moving parts of the machines were not usually covered, serious accidents were common.

▼ The new factories contained rows of clattering machines. They were often very hot and full of fluff or 'lint' from cotton fibres.

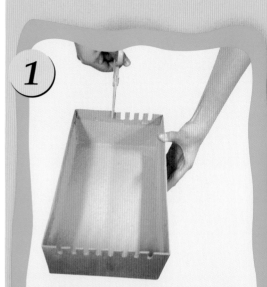

1

With adult help, cut two rows of neat, even grooves opposite each other in the short sides of the shoebox. The grooves should be 0.5cm wide and 1.5cm deep, and spaced 1–2cm apart.

4

Now loop some wool around the threads at both ends of your loom, as shown. This will make sure that the end of your woven cloth is strong and neat.

2

Tape the end of a ball of wool to the base of the box.

3

Wind the wool evenly around the grooves. Make sure the wool is stretched tight. When all the grooves have been used, cut the wool and tape it to the base of the box.

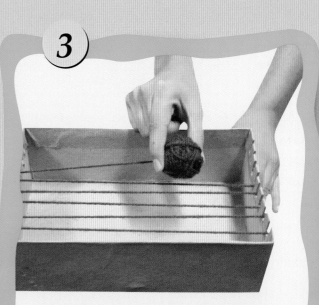

You will need

- Pencil
- Scissors
- Cardboard shoebox
- Wool (in different colours)
- Sticky tape

These long threads are called the warp threads

Make sure the threads are tight before you begin to weave

Turn to pages 14–15 to see how to weave a piece of cloth on the shoebox loom.

How to weave

This part of the project shows you how to weave cloth on the shoebox loom. You can use different coloured wools to create stripes, or you can make your woven fabric from wool of different thicknesses and textures.

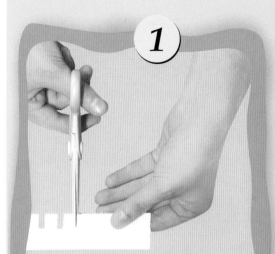

Cut a comb from the lid of the shoebox or a piece of thick card to push down your woven threads. The comb's grooves should fit over the warp threads.

New laws

In the 1800s, laws were passed to improve the terrible working conditions in factories: The 1833 Factory Act banned children under the age of nine from working in factories and mills, and anyone under the age of 18 from working at night.
The 1844 Factory Act made it law that children aged 9–13 should not work more than six and a half hours a day. Children aged 13–18 and women should not work more than 12 hours a day.
The 1847 Ten Hours Act made it law that women and young people must not work more than 10 hours a day in factories.

▲ Huge weaving looms in a factory. By the 1850s, conditions for workers had started to improve but many children still worked six or more hours a day and serious injuries were common.

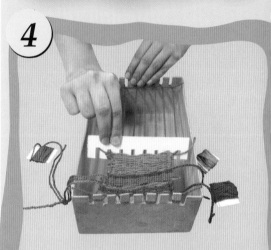

Push back the weft threads with the card comb at the end of each row, to keep them tight and neat. When you have finished weaving, cut the warp threads under the box, and knot the ends.

2

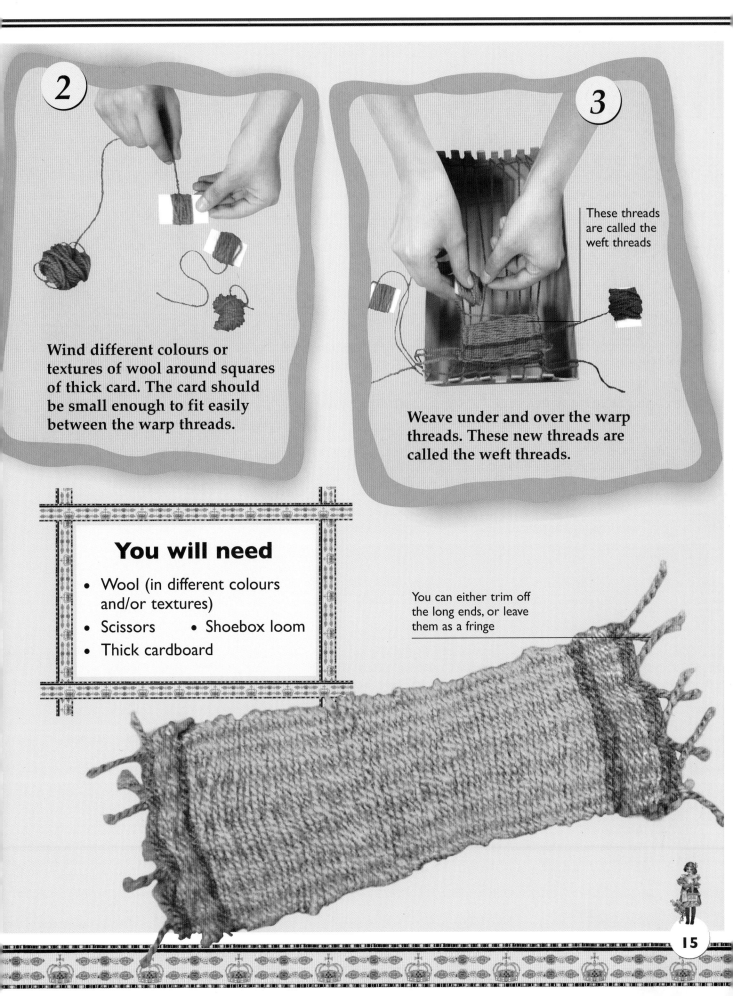

Wind different colours or textures of wool around squares of thick card. The card should be small enough to fit easily between the warp threads.

3

These threads are called the weft threads

Weave under and over the warp threads. These new threads are called the weft threads.

You will need

- Wool (in different colours and/or textures)
- Scissors   • Shoebox loom
- Thick cardboard

You can either trim off the long ends, or leave them as a fringe

Rich lives, poor lives

Victorian Britain was not an equal society. There was a huge difference between the rich and the poor. By the time Queen Victoria died in 1901, there was also a growing middle class of respectable, well-educated lawyers, teachers, doctors and clergymen.

Masters and servants

Wealthy families lived in large, comfortable homes with luxury furnishings and new 'conveniences', such as bathrooms. They were looked after by servants, who cleaned, sewed, cared for children and cooked regular meals. Servants worked hard and had little freedom, but were fed and provided with clothes. In the countryside, farm-workers lived in tumbledown cottages and laboured in all weathers. Poor families ate mostly milk, bread or potatoes.

▲ Public workhouses provided shelter for the poor, in return for hard labour.

◀ Many workers' homes were dark, damp and crowded. Some had rats and bedbugs. Most had no bathrooms, lavatories or running water. Smoke from nearby factories made town air dark and disgusting.

Library
and study

Drawing room, where
family and guests sat,
talked and relaxed.
Families gathered here
to play games and do
hobbies, such as
scrapbooking

▼ Rich Victorians lived in large,
comfortable houses, with many separate
rooms, each for a different activity.

Bathroom
with bath
and flushing
toilet

Dining room,
where family
and guests
ate meals

Comfortable
bedroom for
the couple
who owned
the house

Children's
rooms and
nursery

Servants'
rooms

Impressive
entrance hall

Kitchen, where servants
prepared food

Sick cities

All sorts of criminals, from pickpockets to
muggers and murderers lurked in dark
city streets. In 1829, Sir Robert Peel set up
London's first uniformed police force. It was
copied throughout Britain.

In 1835, town councils were set up in England
and Wales. They collected rates (local taxes),
which paid for street lights, street-cleaning
and fire-fighters.

At the start of Victoria's reign, there were few
drains, sewers or clean water supplies. Polluted
water spread killer diseases, such as typhoid.
From 1848, Boards of Health tried to make
towns cleaner and healthier.

Poor people huddled in damp cellars and
draughty attics; beggars slept in the streets.
In 1875, new laws allowed town councils to
pull down slums and work with charities
to build new housing.

Scrapbooking

In the days before television and computer games, Victorian families entertained themselves by playing card games, such as Happy Families, and board games, such as ludo and snakes and ladders. They also liked to read aloud to each other, or sing songs around the piano. Many women and children kept scrapbooks, in which they glued greetings cards, pressed flowers or messages from their friends as keepsakes.

Cards and scraps

From the mid-1840s, companies began to make and sell Valentine and Christmas cards. These, together with the development of colour printing, led to a huge increase in the popularity of scrapbooking. Many people thought their scrapbook was like a diary in which they kept personal souvenirs and treasures. Valentine and Christmas cards were popular material for scrapbooks. Some Victorian scrapbooks had decorated leather covers with brass locks.

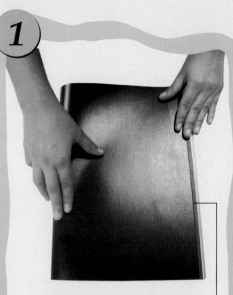

1

Fold six pieces of strong sugar paper or thin card down the middle, then stack them. Fold a thicker piece of card around the outside for a cover.

You can decorate the cover of your scrapbook with pictures or photographs to make it look colourful and attractive

◄ Printed picture sheets (called 'scraps') were produced especially to be pasted into scrapbooks to make attractive patterns. This sheet dates from the 1870s.

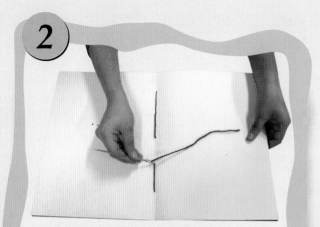

②

Ask an adult to make a hole in the centre of the spine with a darning needle, then make two more holes on either side, equally spaced. Thread the wool or ribbon through the holes, as shown below.

Tie the wool or ribbon in the centre

Your scrapbook

Once you've made your book, you need to decide what to put in it. You might want to make it about your favourite hobby, a sport or a recent holiday. You could include photos, poems, stickers, jokes, programmes or tickets.

Take care arranging the items on each page before you stick them down.

Write captions on pieces of card and glue them alongside each item

Fun and games

By the end of Victoria's reign, new ways of working led to a new industry: organised leisure. Once a year, all the factories in a town closed for a week at the same time, and thousands of workers took a holiday. From 1871, there were also four official bank (public) holidays.

Excursions

At holiday times, many workers travelled by railway train or in charabancs (big coaches, pulled by horses) to enjoy themselves by the sea or in the countryside. They stayed in new, purpose-built hotels, or cheaper lodging houses. New kinds of companies, called travel agents, developed to organise mass travel.

▼ Many new seaside resorts (holiday towns) were built in Victorian Britain. They had hotels, boarding houses, restaurants and theatres.

Long pier (raised walkway, stretching out to sea)

Families on holiday strolled along promenades (paved seaside pathways, with good views)

Punch and Judy (puppet) show

Bathing machine. Queen Victoria went swimming this way

Children played on the sand

Team games

Victorians reorganised old sports and invented new games. Teachers, employers and army commanders all encouraged sports. They said players developed strength, team spirit and leadership skills.

1863 Football Association set up, to organise football games in UK.

1867 Lacrosse comes to Britain (from Canada).

1873 Modern lawn tennis invented.

1871 Rugby Football Union set up.

1875 Official rules for playing hockey established.

1877 First cricket Test Match played between England and Australia.

1877 First tennis tournament at Wimbledon.

1892 Basketball comes to Britain (from USA).

1901 Official rules for playing netball established.

▲ The game of tennis was first played on the grassy lawns of rich Victorian family homes.

New entertainment

By the end of Victoria's reign, most workers were also earning enough to enjoy Saturday night out at a theatre, music hall or public house. On summer Sundays, they might stroll through new city parks and gardens to listen to brass bands.

Ladies carried parasols for protection against the sun

Older people sat on lightweight, folding chairs

◀ An evening out might include going to the circus or to see a travelling show, such as Buffalo Bill's Wild West Exhibition. Many theatres at this time showed a variety of different acts in one show, such as singers, comedians and dancers, that could be enjoyed by the whole family.

Victorian Christmas

New inventions, foreign ideas and Queen Victoria's German husband, Prince Albert, all brought changes to the way Christmas was celebrated. What we think of today as the traditional British Christmas, originated in Victorian times.

Crackers, carols and Santa Claus

At first, Christmas crackers were just fancy wrappings for sweets. But new mass-production methods made it possible to add toys, explosive 'snaps' and mottoes. New Christmas carols, including 'O Little Town of Bethlehem' (1866) and 'Away in a Manger' (1883), soon became well-known, thanks to cheap printing. Roast turkey (replacing goose or beef), Santa Claus (originally St Nicholas, from the Netherlands) and Christmas stockings (hung up for presents) all arrived in Britain from America.

▲ The first Christmas cards were sold in 1843. They were delivered by the newly formed 'Penny Post'.

Many Victorians tried to take some time off work on Christmas Day and Boxing Day (26 December). On both days, rich families believed it was their duty to help the poor.

Christmas trees and their decorations were unknown in Britain until the 1840s, when Prince Albert arranged for them to be brought from Germany to Windsor Castle

There were many street children who had no homes and no parents

Little boy playing a tin whistle

On Boxing Day, the rich rewarded people who worked for them with gifts known as 'Christmas Boxes'

Garland

1 Cut out lots of strips of coloured paper. Each strip should be 4cm wide and either 16 or 20cm long.

2 Glue the ends of one strip together to make a circle. Thread through a second strip and glue the ends. Keep going until you have made a long paper chain.

You will need

- Coloured paper
- Scissors
- Thick card
- Poster paints
- Darning needle
- Gold cord
- PVA glue
- Newspaper
- Glitter

Christmas decorations

1 Cut Christmas shapes out of thick card. Cover each shape with three layers of newspaper, torn into thin strips, and soaked in PVA glue mixed with water.

2 When dry, decorate with poster paints and glitter. Ask an adult to make a hole in the top of each shape with a darning needle, then thread through some gold cord.

New inventions, new discoveries

British engineers, scientists and doctors were world leaders in invention and discovery. Towards the end of Victoria's reign, they also learned from overseas colleagues and rivals, as the Industrial Revolution spread through Europe and America.

Engineering and science

Victorian engineers invented many new materials, from synthetic dyes for fragile silk, to rolled steel plate for warships. They created thousands of new products including safety pins, envelopes, flushing toilets and massive, powerful cranes. Victorian scientists made major discoveries, such as computers, light waves and human evolution. They pioneered medical treatments to save lives: antiseptics killed germs and anaesthetics numbed pain.

▲ For ordinary Victorian people, photographs were a cheaper, more affordable alternative to expensive oil paintings.

Threshing machine

Steam engine

Steam power changed ▶ farming as well as industry. This threshing machine separated ripe grain from wheat stalks. It was powered by a moveable steam engine.

Victorians built huge bridges and tunnels, and laid cables under the Atlantic Ocean to carry electric telegraph messages to the USA.

The Clifton Suspension Bridge, in the west of England, was completed in 1864

Suspension chains support roadway

Tall towers at each end of the bridge support suspension chains

Roadway carries traffic across the River Avon

Gas lamps lit the roadway

Victorians travelled in carriages pulled by horses. Heavy goods were transported in horse-drawn carts

Victorian transport progress

- 1829 First horse-drawn bus, London.
- 1829 Samuel Brown designs a simple internal combustion (petrol) engine.
- 1842 Kirkpatrick Macmillan invents pedal bicycle.
- 1863 First underground railway, pulled by steam locomotives, London.
- 1870–1874 James Starley designs Penny Farthing bicycle, with one big and one small wheel.
- 1885 John Starley designs safety bicycle, with two small, matching wheels.
- 1885 First electric tram, Blackpool
- 1886 Edward Butler designs two-wheeled, two-cylinder (petrol) motorbike.
- 1890 First underground electric 'tube' railway, in London.

Make a zoetrope

In the 1830s, William Fox Talbot discovered a way of taking photographs. This led to the development of cameras that recorded 'still' images, such as family portraits, and then the motion picture camera, in which individual images were stored on a reel. By the end of the 1800s, inventors developed the projector, which projected images from a reel on to a screen, and the 'motion picture' industry was born. An early type of machine that appeared to show moving images was a toy called a zoetrope, invented in 1834. This project shows you how to make your own zoetrope.

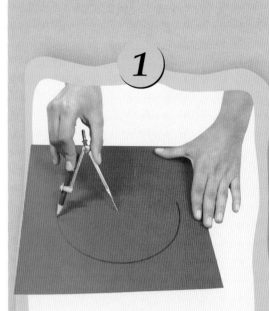

Use a small plate or a pair of compasses to draw a circle on the card. Cut it out, make a hole in the exact centre, then measure the circumference (distance around the edge).

How a zoetrope worked

A zoetrope consisted of a cylinder with a series of slits cut in the side. The viewer placed a strip of pictures in the cylinder, then spun it while looking through the slits. The eye would see one picture at a time but very quickly, making it seem as though the pictures were moving.

A Victorian zoetrope, dating from about 1870, showing an animation of children running. ▶

You will need

- Small plate or pair of compasses
- Cardboard
- Scissors
- Pencil
- Ruler
- Glue
- Paper
- Coloured pens

2

Cut out a strip of card the circumference of your circle, plus an extra 2cm wide and 11cm deep. Cut a row of 10-12 evenly spaced slits, each 5mm wide and 4cm deep, along one edge.

3

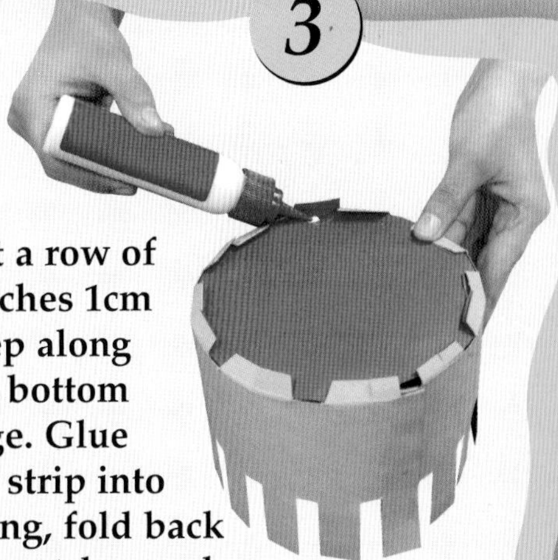

Cut a row of notches 1cm deep along the bottom edge. Glue the strip into a ring, fold back the notches and glue to the circle.

4

Cut out a strip of paper the same width as your card strip and 5cm tall. With a pencil make 10-12 marks on the paper, to match the slits. Draw a row of pictures, one over each pencil mark. Try to make them form a continuous sequence, so the last picture leads on to the first picture.

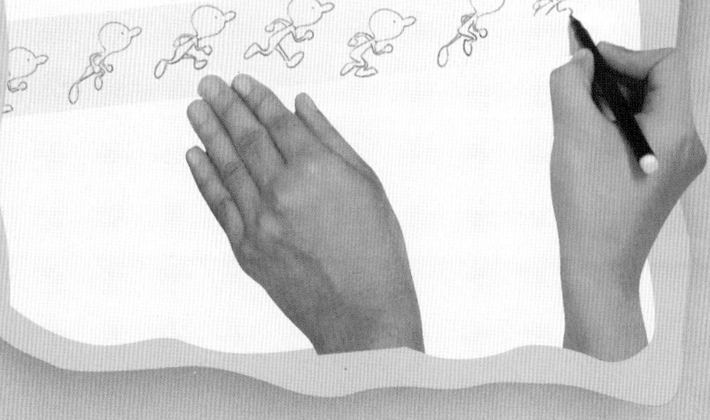

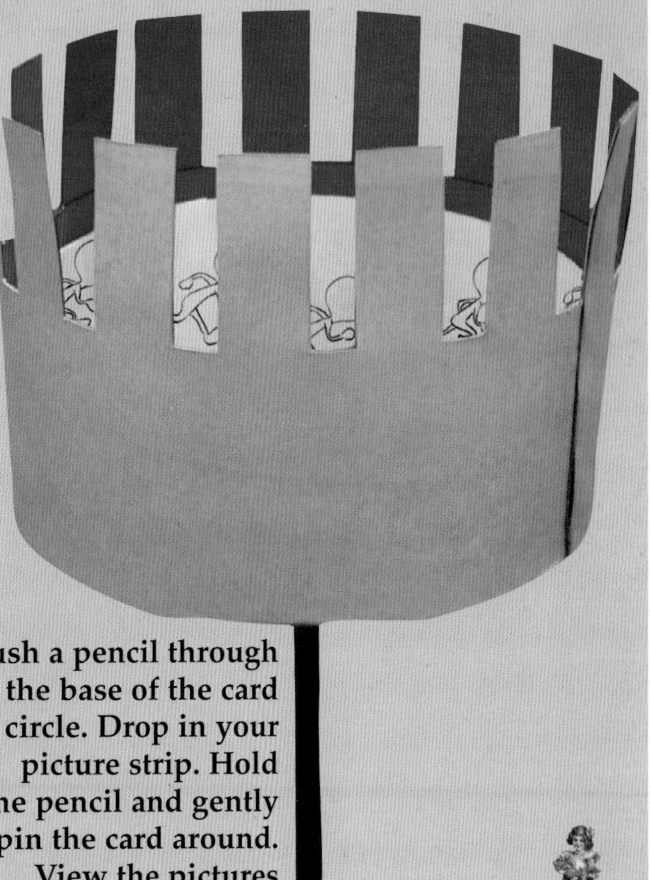

Push a pencil through the base of the card circle. Drop in your picture strip. Hold the pencil and gently spin the card around. View the pictures through the slits.

The British Empire

When young Victoria became queen in 1837, Britain already ruled a large amount of land overseas. During her reign, the British Empire expanded even further.

Britain around the world

Britain took over many foreign lands to obtain valuable raw materials – from cotton and cocoa to diamonds – and to increase British trade. Everywhere they went, British 'empire-builders', such as soldiers, traders, settlers and civil servants, spread the British way of life around the world. They introduced the English language, British-style education, parliaments, sport and laws to many countries.

The Victorians were also great explorers, travelling vast distances to spread Christianity or in search of greater scientific knowledge. Some explorers collected new species of plants and animals, and made collections of them for scientific study and display back home.

VICTORIA QUEEN OF GREAT BRITAIN
EMPRESS OF INDIA
1837—JUBILEE—1887

▲ Queen Victoria pictured at her Golden Jubliee, celebrating 50 years as queen. Victoria wrote in her journal: "No one ever, I believe, has met with such an ovation as was given to me, passing through those six miles of streets. The cheering was quite deafening and every face seemed to be filled with real joy."

The Empire grows

1840 Britain takes control of New Zealand.

1841 Britain takes control of Hong Kong.

1851 Britain controls all Australia.

1857 Britain takes control of India, after Indian troops working for British East India (trading) Company rebel.

1860–1890 'Scramble for Africa'. Britain and other European governments take over African lands.

1876 Queen Victoria becomes Empress of India.

1880–1881 and **1899–1902** Boer Wars. Britain fights Dutch settlers for control of South Africa.

◀ David Livingstone (1813–73) was a missionary and explorer in Africa. He searched for trade routes and campaigned to end the slave trade.

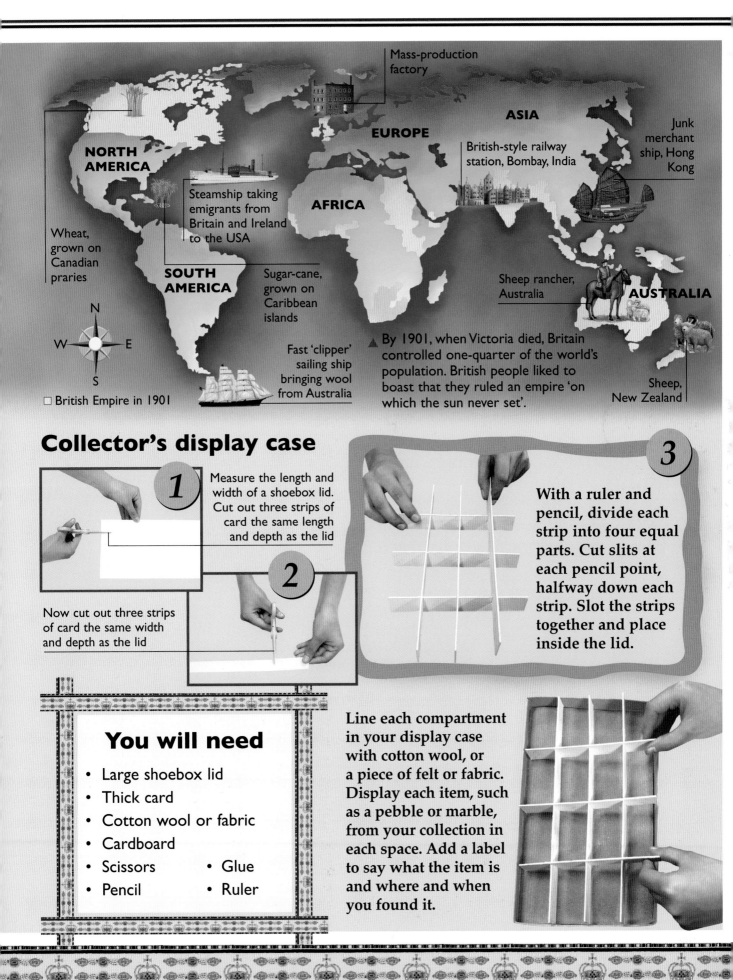

Mass-production factory

ASIA

EUROPE

British-style railway station, Bombay, India

Junk merchant ship, Hong Kong

NORTH AMERICA

Steamship taking emigrants from Britain and Ireland to the USA

AFRICA

Wheat, grown on Canadian praries

SOUTH AMERICA

Sugar-cane, grown on Caribbean islands

Sheep rancher, Australia

AUSTRALIA

N
W · E
S

By 1901, when Victoria died, Britain controlled one-quarter of the world's population. British people liked to boast that they ruled an empire 'on which the sun never set'.

Sheep, New Zealand

□ British Empire in 1901

Fast 'clipper' sailing ship bringing wool from Australia

Collector's display case

1
Measure the length and width of a shoebox lid. Cut out three strips of card the same length and depth as the lid

Now cut out three strips of card the same width and depth as the lid

2

3
With a ruler and pencil, divide each strip into four equal parts. Cut slits at each pencil point, halfway down each strip. Slot the strips together and place inside the lid.

You will need

- Large shoebox lid
- Thick card
- Cotton wool or fabric
- Cardboard
- Scissors
- Glue
- Pencil
- Ruler

Line each compartment in your display case with cotton wool, or a piece of felt or fabric. Display each item, such as a pebble or marble, from your collection in each space. Add a label to say what the item is and where and when you found it.

Timeline

1837 Victoria becomes queen, aged 18.

1840 Victoria marries her first cousin, Albert of Saxe-Coburg-Gotha.

1840s–70s 'Railway Mania' – over 24,000km of tracks built.

1842–78 New laws slowly improve conditions in factories and mines.

1845–48 Irish potato famine. Over a million Irish people die.

1848 First Public Health Act aims to improve living conditions in towns.

1850–1900 Thousands of British families emigrate to the United States, Canada, Australia and New Zealand.

1851 The Great Exhibition in London promotes British trade and inventions.

1854–56 Crimean War between Britain and Russia. Florence Nightingale nurses wounded soldiers, but almost 20,000 die.

1857 Indian soldiers rebel; Britain takes control of India.

1861 Prince Albert dies; Queen Victoria hides from the public for 13 years.

1869 Suez Canal opens, linking Mediterranean Sea and Indian Ocean. Voyages to India and empire lands in Asia and the Pacific become much shorter.

1870 Primary education provided for all children.

1876 Alexander Graham Bell (Scots/American engineer, working in USA) invents telephone.

1882 New laws allow married women to own money and property.

1884 Safety (low, two-wheeled) bicycle invented. Ordinary men can now travel much further and more quickly, to work or for relaxation. By 1901, some women become cyclists, as well.

1884 Third Reform Act. Most ordinary men now have the right to vote.

1886 and 1893 Irish nationalists call for Home Rule (independence).

1897 Queen Victoria celebrates Diamond Jubilee (60 years reign).

1899–1902 Britain wins Second Boer War.

1901 Queen Victoria dies.

Glossary

Bathing machine A small, private room on wheels, from which bathers stepped out into the sea.

Bedbugs Insects that live in walls, floors and furnishings. They suck human blood.

Blast furnace A huge oven used to produce iron from ore (rock) by heating it with coke, limestone and blasts of air.

Charabanc A horse-drawn coach carrying many passengers.

Chartist A member of a group that campaigned for political and social reform, 1836–1848.

Co-operative A trade organisation of people working together and sharing the profits.

Conveniences Inventions that make life easier or more pleasant.

Excursion A holiday or day trip.

Mass-production Making very large numbers of identical objects by machine, quickly and cheaply.

Monarch A king or queen.

Organ grinder A street musician who played a small, portable instrument, called a barrel-organ.

Penny post The British uniform postal service, which began in 1840. A single penny stamp paid for a letter or card to be delivered anywhere in Britain.

Pier A raised walkway, stretching out to sea. Often with buildings for entertainment, such as concert halls or restaurants.

Promenade A paved seaside pathway, with good views.

Punch and Judy A show featuring glove puppets. The main characters are Mr Punch and his long-suffering wife, Judy.

Workhouse A big building, almost like a prison, where very poor people were taken. They had to work and obey orders in return for food and shelter.

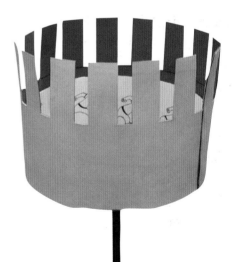

Index

Webfinder

http://www.bbc.co.uk/schools/victorians/index.shtml
Interactive site about children in Victorian Britain.

http://www.bbc.co.uk/history/british/victorians/victorian_technology_01.shtml
Lots of information about inventions and technology in the Victorian age.

http://www.learningcurve.gov.uk/snapshots/snapshot03/snapshot3.htm
Fascinating facts revealed by Queen Victoria's family photograph. Scroll down the web-page for links to other very useful sites.

http://www.learningcurve.gov.uk/victorianbritain/industrial/default.htm
What was life in Victorian Britain really like? Find out from archive photos and old documents.

http://www.bbc.co.uk/history/british/victorians/speed_01.shtml
Britain at the end of the Victorian age.